KFK KINGFISHER KNOWLEDGE

FORENSICS

Officers search a car park for evidence after a shooting. To ensure that nothing is overlooked, the police have formed a line, standing shoulder to shoulder. Each officer then searches the area directly in front of him.

FORENSICS

Richard Platt

Foreword by
Kathy Reichs

KINGFISHER

Editor: Jennifer Schofield
Senior designer: Carol Ann Davis
Picture research manager: Cee Weston-Baker
DTP manager: Nicky Studdart
Senior production controller: Lindsey Scott
Proofreader and indexer: Sheila Clewley
Consultant: Dr C H Steele, Principal Lecturer:
 Forensic Science, London South Bank University

KINGFISHER

Kingfisher Publications Plc
New Penderel House
283–288 High Holborn
London WC1V 7HZ
www.kingfisherpub.com

First published by
Kingfisher Publications Plc 2005
1TR/0605/TWP/MA(MA)/130ENSOMA/F

10 9 8 7 6 5 4 3 2 1
Printed in Singapore
Copyright © Kingfisher Publications Plc 2005
ISBN-13: 978 0 7534 1113 1
ISBN-10: 0 7534 1113 X

Contents

GO FURTHER...
INFORMATION PANEL KEY:

websites and
further reading

career paths

places to visit

CHAPTER 3

CRIME LAB 39

Foreword

Do you ever watch police shows on TV? Or read mystery stories? Ever think you'd be good at catching the bad guys? If so, this book is just for you!

Contrary to popular thinking, police cases are not cracked by glamour, or by razzle-dazzle techno-wizardry. Nor are they cracked by heroes working solo. Law enforcement relies on careful evidence collection, skilled detective work, and good old science. It is through teamwork that investigators learn what happened at a crime scene and who was there. Forensic scientists make up an important part of every police team.

Forensics is packed with information about forensic scientists. It describes what we do in terms of two broad categories: field work (collecting evidence) and laboratory work (analyzing evidence).

Back in the early 1900s, Dr Edmond Locard was the director of a police laboratory in Lyon, France. He thought up a rule that still bears his name. Locard's Exchange Principle says that every contact leaves a trace. That means that every time people meet, or touch, or even enter a room they leave tiny specks of themselves behind, and they carry tiny specks off when they go. Maybe a thread, a dust particle, or even an eyelash. It is those transferred specks that sink the bad guys.

Scene of crime investigators go to a crime scene and seal it off. They video and photograph the setting and the victim (if there is one). These men and women are trained to spot Locard's tiny specks, and to see patterns between things. They know how to collect and preserve fingerprints, blood, tyre tracks, paint chips, or bullet fragments. Even that dust particle or eyelash that was left behind!

The crime scene workers take everything they have collected to the crime laboratory. There, each scientist examines something different. Some focus on documents and writing. Some look at tools and weapons, or chemicals and poisons, or bombs and explosives, or DNA and other biological substances.

For many years I have worked at a combination crime and medico-legal lab in Montreal. I am on the medico-legal side. Our section has a specific task. The 'evidence' we examine is the victim. Sometimes our job is to identify a body. Sometimes our job is to figure out how or why someone died.

Like those in the crime lab, the scientists in the medico-legal section also have speciality areas. The forensic pathologist performs autopsies to determine the cause of death. The forensic dentist examines teeth. The forensic radiologist studies X-rays.

I am a forensic anthropologist. I examine decomposed, burned and mummified bodies, and skeletons. I may be asked to determine someone's age, sex, race and height. I may be asked to look for injuries in their bones. I may be asked to estimate how long someone has been dead, or to describe what was done to their body after they stopped breathing.

I love being a forensic scientist. It is rewarding and exciting work. I help families gain peace by providing answers. I help police solve crimes by providing clues. I help prosecutors in court by providing testimony.

Forensics is a terrific introduction to my world. The chapters and photographs explain what my colleagues and I do at the crime scene and in the crime lab. The book shows just how cool science can be.

Forensic science is a hot topic with the media right now. That won't last. It doesn't matter. Crime will always be with us. Forensic scientists will always be needed. I hope this book inspires you to join our team.

Kathy Reichs

Kathy Reichs – International best-selling crime writer and forensic anthropologist

CHAPTER 1

Signs of the crime

Every minute of every day, criminals are at work. To catch them, police forces rely more and more on forensic science – the science of solving crime.

Forensic science starts at the crime scene, the place where a crime is committed. There, investigators hope to find clues that will lead them to a suspect: someone who may have carried out the crime. They search the crime scene for evidence. This is any object, mark or pattern that can provide them with information about the crime.

By photographing, studying and testing the evidence, forensic scientists can link suspects to a crime scene, and help prove whether they are guilty or innocent.

The crime scene

Blue lights flash around a dark street. Striped plastic tape flaps between trees. Uniformed figures keep back a curious crowd. Welcome to a crime scene. Law officers and detectives take special care to preserve crime scenes exactly as they find them, because evidence is fragile, and clumsy feet and prying hands can easily destroy it. Without evidence, it may be impossible to solve a crime and catch the villains who carried it out.

One and only chance

The first officers to arrive at the scene of a crime must take a careful look around but avoid disturbing anything that they find. There are very good reasons for this caution and care: the first officers to arrive have a special, once-only chance because they see the crime scene completely fresh and untouched. Very soon, their own actions – and those of others – will make changes that can never be undone. For example, just walking across a carpet to help an injured person can destroy the footprints of a fleeing attacker.

Preserving evidence

Scene of crime officers (SOCOs) take steps quickly to protect and preserve the crime scene. They look to see where criminals might have entered before committing the crime – and how they left afterwards. These places may hold important clues, such as the suspect's fingerprints, so it is vital that they remain untouched. Scene of crime officers also try to guess where they will *not* find evidence. They will use only these areas to enter and leave the crime scene, so that they do not disturb other, more important places.

Securing the scene

Once the crime scene is taped off, there are other simple, but essential, precautions that officers need to take. They must not eat, drink or smoke, because these activities leave traces that may later confuse investigators. For the same reason, they must not use the phone or the lavatory if they are part of the crime scene. Sometimes, their work forces them to make a change to the crime scene – such as opening a door to enter. If this happens, they make a written note recording that the door was shut when they arrived. Details like this can make the difference between a villain going to jail and escaping unpunished.

Vital witnesses

For all their careful observation and note-taking, officers can never know as much about a crime as someone who actually saw it happen. These witnesses are vital to an investigation. Police race to identify them, and make sure that they do not leave the crime scene before being interviewed.

◄ When police officers respond to an emergency call, their first jobs are to care for any victims of the crime, arrest suspects (shown left), and identify witnesses (the people who saw the crime).

► The more people who visit a crime scene, the more chance there is of destroying evidence. So an important priority is to keep away journalists, curious neighbours — and even other officials whose visit is not absolutely essential. Uniformed officers do this by ringing the crime scene with 'do not cross' tape and putting an officer on guard.

► All evidence found and interviews with eye-witnesses are logged and recorded in police files. Laptop technology and wireless communication enable officers to access files from police headquarters while at a crime scene. This allows them to cross-reference information quickly and easily.

Collecting evidence

Clues that investigators find at a crime scene can lead them to the criminals who are responsible for the crime. However, a thorough search for evidence is important even when the police officers are certain that they know who did it. Without evidence, it is hard to prove that the suspect was even at the crime scene. And, in a court of law, a judge or jury may doubt what the police tell them if there is no evidence. Unless it is certain that suspects are guilty, they cannot be punished.

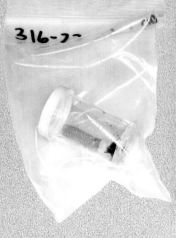

▲ The index number and description of each piece of evidence are stored on a database. This enables officers to keep track of all evidence.

Scene of crime officers

It is the SOCOs' job to search for, preserve and record evidence. For example, a broken window might show how burglars entered a house. Blood on the window can help identify them and fingerprints may match a known criminal's record. However, few crimes are this straightforward. Skilled criminals take care not to leave such obvious clues. Even if the explanation of the crime seems clear, and investigators believe they know who did it, they must still record everything.

Starting the search

SOCOs begin by searching for evidence that time or weather might destroy – tyre tracks in snow, for example. Then they look at the areas that are associated with the crime. For example, in murder cases they search near the body.

Knowing where to look

SOCOs also look in less obvious places. For example, a suspect reaching to take something from a shelf might avoid touching the shelf itself. But, because right-handed people unconsciously reach out for support with their left hand, SOCOs look for fingerprint evidence on surfaces to the left.

▼ Clean, disposable gloves are used to take samples of dried blood for laboratory analysis. SOCOs wear disposable paper suits to ensure that any evidence they find is not from their own clothes.

Looking everywhere

So that they miss no details, SOCOs make sure their search covers the whole crime scene. In a house, they list the rooms and search each in turn. Outdoors, they might stand shoulder to shoulder, and walk forwards in a line, or start in the centre and spiral out to the edges.

Bag, seal and label

Before evidence is removed, it is photographed (see pages 12–13) and its location is plotted on a plan. Then, taking care that it is not altered in any way, it is bagged, sealed and labelled. A record is made of what has been found, who found it and where it was found. This log grows every time anyone studies or moves the evidence. Called the 'chain of custody', it enables officers to prove that nobody has tampered with evidence.

▶ The closeness of the search depends on what SOCOs are looking for and the size of the crime scene. If it is small, they kneel and search with their fingertips.

Photography

Cameras are perhaps the detective's most useful tool at the crime scene. With a simple snapshot camera, forensic photographers can make a quick record before anything is disturbed by a search for evidence. However, it is not always as simple as it seems. Sophisticated equipment and special lighting techniques are used to show clues that are invisible to the naked eye. Cameras also capture evidence that is too big to remove from the crime scene, and traces that later tests may destroy.

▲ Alphonse Bertillon was the first to realize that photographs are useless for identification unless they all use the same lighting and angle. Here Bertillon himself poses for the front-and-side views of the now standard police 'mug shot' he pioneered.

▼ Special forensic light sources create intense beams of brilliant colours. Used with special chemicals, these shafts of light make fingerprints stand out more clearly in photographs, or reveal washed-away blood stains.

First photographs

As long ago as 1843 – just four years after the invention of photography – Belgian police began taking pictures of known criminals. In France, chief of criminal identification, Alphonse Bertillon (1853–1914), pioneered the use of photography to solve crime. He made detectives take pictures in a scientific way, with matching lighting and camera angles to make comparison easier. He also insisted that they include a scale, such as a ruler, so that it was easy to judge the size of objects in the final print.

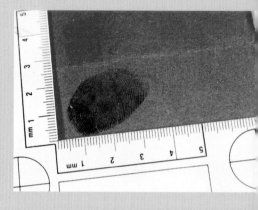

▲ Including a scale in forensic close-up photographs enables detectives to judge the size of the object in the picture. For fingerprints size is usually obvious, but for other objects, such as knives, size is less clear – and very important.

Lining up the picture

Some of Bertillon's ideas are in use today. Forensic photographers still include a scale. They also make sure that the camera is positioned exactly in line with the subject, rather than on a slant. These precautions ensure that the camera records the evidence as clearly as possible.

However, the technology and equipment that photographers use has changed. Today they use colour pictures, and – with digital cameras or instant film – they can see whether they have the picture they want.

▶ Whether photographers are using film or digital, the methods they use are similar. Much of their work consists of making a simple record of the crime scene from all angles. For this they use equipment and methods that are hardly any different from those we use for holiday snaps.

Taking close-ups

When taking close-ups of evidence, detectives need sharp images, with plenty of detail. They often light the scene to make the picture clearer, and include a scale bar. For example, evidence that is raised or pressed into a surface, such as a tyre track in mud, is not always easy to see. Placing a light at one side of the camera casts strong shadows that make the pattern stand out.

Special lights

Other evidence only shows up with special lighting. Ultraviolet radiation can make fingerprints, sweat and urine glow. Scrubbed-away blood stains also glow under purple light if they are sprayed with a special chemical (see page 20).

Tell-tale marks

A trail of blood, a cluster of bullet holes or a series of scratches on a window ledge: all of these marks at a crime scene have a story to tell. They are all forms of pattern evidence. Reading and understanding them helps detectives to reconstruct a crime. The shape of the marks and their position can show the way a villain broke into a house, where a killer was standing, and even whether they were right- or left-handed!

▲ Patterns of blood tell a story of violent crime. The shape and size of the blood spots show how far the blood flew or fell, and the direction in which it was travelling. Blood pools on the ground tell detectives where a victim lay injured or dying. They are numbered to help detectives describe the crime scene.

Putting marks together

Individual marks in pattern evidence may not be important in themselves: for example, a single groove in a window frame might tell investigators very little. But taken together, all the marks that make up the pattern say much more. These scratches and indentations are called toolmarks. For example, marks made by a tool when forcing open a door can be matched back to the tool.

The nicks that say 'you're nicked!'

Sometimes, toolmarks show only what kind of tool the criminal used. However, worn tools have scratches and nicks that make them like no other. When an old crowbar is used to lever open a window, the tool presses into the paintwork a pattern that is as unique as a signature. If police find the crowbar, they can compare its marks with the pattern evidence, and accuse its owner.

Arms and ammunition

Guns also tell a story – or even two, because there are two parts to each bullet. The lead slug fired from the barrel marks or pierces everything it strikes. This pattern shows detectives how the bullet flew. The other part of the bullet, the cartridge case, does not fly down the barrel. Instead, it is usually ejected to one side. So the pattern of cases can show where an assassin was standing to shoot.

◄ The pattern of cracks in shattered windows shows not only where the bullets flew, but also the order in which they were fired. The cracks from each bullet will not cross a crack caused by a bullet fired earlier.

▶ Careful burglars wear gloves to avoid leaving fingerprints, but the tools they use to force their way in may also leave a pattern that can lead detectives to them.

Charting patterns

Investigators at the crime scene use measurements and cameras to gather and preserve pattern evidence. For example, where a shooting has taken place, detectives mark the position of the ejected cartridge cases with numbered tabs, and photograph them before collecting them for analysis (see page 54). To document a bullet's flight they retrace it with cord, rods or laser beams.

Analyzing blood marks is a special skill. Detectives chart the angles of splattered drops using ruled lines, threads or a computer. The drops literally point to where the victim was standing when they were wounded.

Guns, blood and tools are not the only things that leave tell-tale patterns. Broken glass, burns and furniture may leave marks that an alert detective can use to solve a crime.

◀ Laser beams are a convenient way to follow the path of a bullet from the gun barrel to the victim, but they do not show up on normal photographs. Filling the scene with smoke reveals the laser beam as a vivid coloured line, and may show the likely direction for the recovery of the bullet if it missed its intended victim.

Finding a body

Suspicious deaths are a special challenge for investigators. Since murder is the most serious of crimes, they need to take extraordinary care to preserve any evidence they might find on or around the body. Even the temperature of the body itself is important because it can show when the victim died. However, the first step is to make sure that the 'corpse' is actually dead, so investigators always check for signs of life – even if this means destroying clues.

Looking for signs of life

Investigators look for breathing and a pulse. If the victim shows these 'vital signs', investigators call an ambulance and start first aid.

If there are no signs of life, there is little that investigators can do except await the arrival of a forensic pathologist and a photographer. Pathologists are medical doctors who study diseases and injuries and their causes. Forensic pathologists specialize in the harm that crime does to the human body.

◀ Throughout the examination, the forensic photographer is at the pathologist's elbow. The two work as a team to record the death scene as precisely as possible. Together, their notes and pictures form an important link in the chain of evidence that they hope will convict the killer.

Time of death

Before the pathologist touches the corpse, the photographer takes several pictures of it. This is necessary because the pathologist's examination will alter the crime scene and may change some of the evidence.

To work out when a person died, the pathologist takes the body's core temperature and that of the air. When the air is at 21°C, bodies cool by about 10°C in 12 hours, so these two measurements show the time of death.

▶ Although the skin of a corpse feels cold, the body's core cools more slowly than the outside. In this picture, taken with a camera that records temperature differences with colour, you can see that the warmest regions, tinted purple, are in the middle of the body.

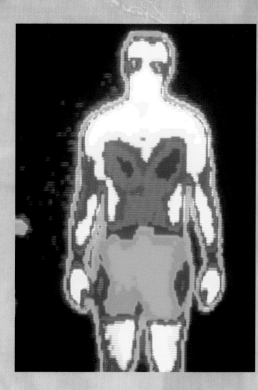

Deadly stiffness

Next, the pathologist checks for rigor mortis (death stiffness) which makes limbs hard to move. It starts in the face, then spreads to the whole body in 6–12 hours. How far it has spread can indicate time of death.

The pathologist also conducts a brief general examination of the body, looking only for evidence that may decay or disappear. Samples are taken from the mouth and the body's other openings. Some fluids may already have drained out; samples from the soil, floor or furniture on which the victim lies confirm this.

Tell-tale tint

The pathologist also looks for red colouring. After death, blood drains to the lower half of the body, giving it a pinker colour. If this is anywhere else, the corpse may have been moved.

Finally, the body is taken to the laboratory. Within the body bag, an extra layer of wrapping is placed on the head, hands and feet. This makes it easier to identify and collect evidence that falls from these body parts.

◣ In hunts for missing people and victims of violent crimes, police use specially trained tracker dogs as early in the investigation as they can. As the investigation expands, large numbers of searchers — often both police and volunteers — get involved. Their scents spread across the search area, confusing the dogs.

Lifting prints

One very special kind of pattern evidence has unique value to investigators. Fingerprints are the most personal of all patterns, and we leave them on almost everything we touch. They are formed by the whirling ridges on the skin of our hands. Everyone has a different pattern of ridges. The fingerprints criminals leave behind can prove where they have been, what they have done – and most important of all, who they are.

▲ A roll of sticky tape is all it takes to lift prints from shiny objects at the crime scene. The glue holds prints firmly on an evidence card.

The personal touch

Investigators look very carefully for fingerprints. Sometimes they are obvious, but more often, villains do not make the detective's work easy. The prints that clean hands leave, even on glossy surfaces such as glass or metal, are hard to see unless the light shines from just the right angle. On rougher and patterned surfaces, such as paper, fingerprints may be completely invisible.

Latent prints

To find these hidden or 'latent' prints on glossy surfaces, SOCOs use dusting brushes to coat the surfaces criminals may have touched with very fine powder. The powder sticks to traces of grease and sweat that mark the fingerprints. To avoid smudging prints on very shiny surfaces, officers use powder mixed with iron dust, applying it with a magnetic brush that does not touch the surface.

Recording the marks

The next step is to preserve the prints so they can be used as evidence. First SOCOs take photographs of the prints. Then, if the object is small enough, they remove it to the crime lab, taking care not to disturb the prints. If the prints are on an object that cannot be moved, they lift them with special sticky tape. By sticking the tape to an evidence card, SOCOs ensure they can file it and find it again

◄ Detectives looking for fingerprint evidence start in the obvious places. At home, nobody wears gloves to type, so this officer is dusting a computer keyboard.

Casting deep prints

Fingerprints are not the only prints that investigators study at crime scenes. They also look for the prints left by bare feet and shoes, and for the tracks of vehicle tyres.

Officers at the crime scene record deeply pressed footprints, shoeprints, ear-prints and tyre tracks, first with a camera, then by pouring a liquid casting compound into the hollow of the print. This sets into a solid lump in minutes, creating a permanent record that detectives can match with the feet, shoes or vehicle of a suspect.

Footprints and shoeprints left on a carpet or floor are more difficult to record. Often, if the prints are hard to photograph, SOCOs try to lift them.

▲ Tyre tracks at a road traffic accident enable investigators to reconstruct what happened. They can show how fast each vehicle was moving, which way each driver was turning the steering wheel, and when they applied the brakes.

To do this, there are several different devices that can be used. On hard floors, officers use gel – a sheet of tacky material that picks up the pattern in the dust or dirt. If there are prints left on documents or paper, officers use an electrostatic lifter. This is a foil sheet coated in black plastic connected to a device that generates a high-static electric charge. The static charge draws the dust from the print on to the black plastic, where it is seen more easily.

▼ Shoeprints from trainers are valuable evidence because no two styles have the same tread pattern. Matching style alone is not enough to prove that a suspect's shoes left prints at the crime scene: wear marks and cuts in the soles must also match.

Showing up the invisible

At the scene of a bloody murder, the killer is hard at work cleaning up. Buckets of detergent erase all the stains of the horrible crime that happened here… or do they? When investigators come calling, they are suspicious. They spray the crime scene with special chemicals – and a pattern of glowing bloodstains appears on the walls and floor. It sounds like magic, but it is pure forensic science. Detectives have a large and growing tool kit of chemicals and methods that make hidden clues visible.

Searching for blood

Signs of crimes are not always easy to see. Investigators have to work hard to find the clues they need to catch criminals and prove their guilt.

Detectives need to know whether there is any blood at a crime scene and where it is. To find out, they spray any suspicious areas with chemicals, such as luminol or fluorescein. These two chemicals make bloodstains glow in the dark and, even after scrubbing, there is still enough blood left to make the chemicals react. Although luminol glows for only a few seconds after spraying, fluorescein produces a longer-lasting glow when the stains are lit with a beam of ultraviolet light.

Revealing fingerprints

Just as these chemicals can reveal faint bloodstains, so others can show up weak prints on surfaces that are difficult or impossible to dust.

One of the best ways to make prints easier to see, is to use cyanoacrylate adhesive or superglue. This gives off a vapour that sticks to sweat in fingerprints, and coats each line of the print with a hard, white plastic layer that shows up clearly. Detectives fumigate surfaces that might have fingerprints with superglue fumes, or take small objects to the crime lab to process them in a fume-filled box.

◀ When used with dusts and dyes, laser light makes otherwise invisible prints show up clearly. Detectives wear coloured goggles to protect their eyes, and to make the prints appear clearer.

Problem prints

Wet or absorbent surfaces need different treatments. Ninhydrin, which is used on surfaces such as wallpaper, turns the sweat in fingerprints purple. DFO works in a similar way. It is 100 times more sensitive, but needs an ultraviolet light to show up the prints.

The case of Richard Rogers

Plastic bags dumped beside roads in New England, USA in the 1990s hid grisly secrets: five men's bodies cut into pieces. Police were baffled for nearly ten years, until forensic scientists found a new way to make invisible fingerprints show up on plastic. Vacuum metal deposition (VMD) used gold vapour to reveal prints as clearly as a photograph. Comparing fingerprints from the bags with records from every US state led detectives to New York nurse Richard Rogers. Gloves found with one body had been bought near his home. Rogers was arrested in 2001.

◀ The difference that fingerprint enhancement techniques make is obvious in this two-part picture. The right-hand side shows the faint print before it was sprayed with special chemicals. The left-hand side shows how clearly every ridge can be seen after being treated with chemicals.

▶ The bright glow from enhanced fingerprints is called fluorescence. Fluorescent substances like this laboratory chemical absorb invisible radiation and convert its energy to coloured light that we can see and photograph.

SUMMARY OF CHAPTER 1: SIGNS OF THE CRIME

Clues at the scene

Investigators search the crime scene for evidence that might lead them to the person who committed the crime. If they cannot collect evidence immediately, they protect it until it can be safely recorded. They also care for any victims, and interview witnesses. Scene of crime officers (SOCOs) make notes, measure and take pictures of any evidence. Crime scene photographers use special lighting techniques to photograph faint details. They may use digital cameras so they can see results instantly.

Patterns of evidence

Usually, the patterns of evidence reveal more than individual pieces. For example, blood spots tell SOCOs about the weapon used, and patterns from bullets show where a killer stood, and how the bullet flew.

Fingerprints are a special kind of pattern evidence. Everyone's fingertips are different, so their prints are a useful way of identification. However, fingerprints are not easy to see. Detectives make them clearer by dusting with powder. Photographing the prints or lifting them

with sticky tape preserves them. Detectives also record footprints and tyre prints on soft ground by casting impressions. They lift dusty prints from documents with a special electrostatic mat. Investigators even have ways to find invisible marks. They use chemical sprays and UV lights to make scrubbed-away blood show up.

Corpses

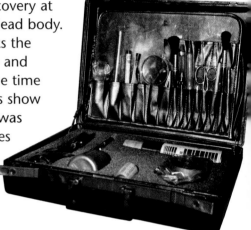

The most grisly discovery at a crime scene is a dead body. A pathologist checks the body's temperature and stiffness to judge the time of death. Red marks show whether the body was moved, and samples of body fluids are taken too, before the body is sent to the laboratory.

Go further...

To find out more about the various disciplines of forensic science, and play a detective game, visit: http://library.thinkquest.org/17049/gather/index.en.shtml

Find the clues and solve the mystery of the barefoot burglar at: http://www.cyberbee.com/whodunnit/crimescene.html

Take a virtual field trip and find out more about the FBI and how they solve crimes: http://www.fbi.gov/kids/k5th/kidsk5th.htm

Eyewitness Crime & Detection by Brian Lane (DK 1998)

Crime scene manager
Controls the crime scene, supervizes SOCOs, gives information to news media, and communicates with police headquarters.

Evidence assistant
Receives, tracks and catalogues evidence from the crime scene, and makes sure it is available at trial.

Forensic imaging specialist
Carries out photography and video at the crime scene, often using special lighting techniques.

Scene of crime officer (SOCO)
Protects the crime scene, collects and preserves evidence, takes fingerprints, and documents the scene.

Travel through three centuries of crime and punishment, reliving the lives, trials and executions of some of Nottingham's most notorious criminals. Crack the case and use forensics to help solve the crimes: Nottingham Galleries of Justice, Shire Hall, High Pavement, Nottingham, NG1 1HN, UK Telephone: +44 (0) 115 952 0555 www.galleriesofjustice.org.uk

Check out fingerprints, hair, footprints and ink in the laboratory to find out which villain committed the crime: Newcastle Life Science Centre, Times Square, Newcastle Upon Tyne, NE1 4EP, UK Telephone: +44 (0) 191 243 8223 www.lifesciencecentre.co.uk

14:53:06

14:53:47

14:54:18

14:54:57

CCTV images show a car thief at work

CHAPTER 2

Who is it?

Yᵒu are unique! This is not a compliment, but a simple fact. Each human is different from every other.

However, knowing that everyone is different is not the same as showing it. When detectives want to identify a criminal or a victim, they have to find all the things about a person that make them different from others.

The surest way to do this is with DNA analysis: a study of the human body's biological 'master plan'. However, this is slow and expensive. Comparing a face to a photograph is perhaps the easiest way, but is surprisingly unreliable. Fingerprints are such a sensitive test of identity that they can even prove that 'identical' twins are different people.

Evidence from blood

Pumping through our veins, or collecting in a vivid red pool, blood can show detectives exactly who we are – or who we used to be when we were alive. Blood and other body fluids, such as saliva, are so important to forensic science that their study has its own name: serology. Serologists have developed a wide range of identity tests. DNA testing is the newest, but other tests have been around for a century.

Different types of blood

Blood is our life-fluid: if we lose too much, we could die. Doctors have known this for centuries, but when they tried to 'top up' lost blood with blood given by a healthy person, often, their patients died. Biologist Karl Landsteiner (1868–1943) found out why. He showed that people have different kinds of blood. Most of us have one of four types, which he called type A, B, AB and O.

Blood tests

In 1902, Landsteiner helped devise a 'blood typing' test for blood stains. This showed the group to which a stain belonged, so he suggested that detectives could use the test to solve crimes. For instance, they could test blood stains found on a murder suspect's clothes and compare them to the blood of the victim. Matching the two blood types would help to prove the suspect's guilt.

However, because out of every ten people, roughly four have type 'A' blood and five have type 'O', the test was not a very accurate way of proving a suspect's guilt. It was much better, though, at proving innocence. If the blood-soaked clothes did not match the victim's blood, police could be sure the suspect did not commit the crime. Today, when investigators find blood at a crime scene, they still use the 'ABO test' to eliminate suspects. However, before they do this, they carry out even simpler tests.

◄ The ABO blood test uses two test solutions called antibodies. 'Anti-A' solution makes type A blood cells form clumps. Type B blood clumps with 'Anti-B'. AB type blood clumps with both, and type O with neither.

▼ Our bodies contain five or six litres (ten pints) of blood. But to identify a suspect, serologists need just one forty-millionth of a drop (shown here greatly magnified).

▶ To analyze blood, technicians first use spotlessly clean instruments to carefully remove the stain. Then they moisten it with salt water to make a liquid sample for testing.

Is it really blood?

The first of these tests is what forensic detectives call a presumptive test for blood. It shows whether or not it is safe to presume that a stain really is blood. This is not as silly as it sounds: blood is not always easy to recognize, and is easy to confuse with other substances.

Spraying for evidence

The luminol and fluorescein sprays (see page 20) that detectives use to spot blood stains are themselves presumptive tests, but there are many other tests that can be used.

The easiest to use are Hemastix – small tabs with a test chemical at one end. Investigators at the crime scene moisten the stick and rub it on the stain. If it is blood, the tip of the Hemastix turns from yellow to green.

Blood or sauce?

Though these tests are a great help to detectives looking for blood at the crime scene, they do not provide all the answers. Horseradish, for example, contains chemicals similar to blood, so a stain that passes a presumptive test for blood may in fact turn out to be the remains of roast dinner.

Technicians in a serology laboratory prepare samples for testing. One of the first checks is to determine if the blood is human. Serologists use the precipitin test for this. Dropped into a test tube, or forced across a piece of sticky jelly by an electric current, the sample forms a clear line where it meets the test chemical.

DNA analysis

The police charge a shoplifter and take a mouth swab to analyze his DNA. Although the thief has not been arrested before, they find it matches DNA from the scene of a brutal, unsolved murder committed many years earlier. When they question the thief, he breaks down and admits to the killing. It sounds like a detective's dream, but it is happening now. Invented in 1984, DNA analysis has become a key weapon in the fight against crime.

▲ Identical twins do not just look similar. They really are exactly the same — down to the last gene. DNA analysis cannot tell them apart, but can easily distinguish between ordinary siblings.

Genes and DNA

Within the cells of our bodies there is a tiny strand of protein called DNA – deoxyribonucleic acid. Half our DNA, called genes, comes from each of our parents – this is why we look like them.

Genes make up only part of our DNA – the rest is regular patterns of protein. These also come from our parents, but the number of times they are repeated is unique to each person. Because our DNA is unique, but similar to our relatives, it is a useful method of identifying people.

Extracting DNA

If investigators at the crime scene find a spot of blood or spit, the crime lab can extract DNA from it. Comparing the extracted DNA with the suspect's can confirm whether or not they were involved in the crime – or even whether the suspect's mother or son was involved.

To make the comparison, the lab first extracts DNA and mixes it with special chemicals that multiply the repeated patterns until there is enough material to test.

Racing for a result

Next, technicians mark each repeated pattern with a dye, and 'race' the strands down a narrow tube. A sensor at the tube's far end identifies each coloured strand and feeds the data into a computer. The results form a DNA profile, or 'fingerprint', that identifies who the sample came from.

The final stage is to compare the results to a suspect's DNA sample. If there is no suspect, detectives look for a match in a computer file of the DNA profiles of known criminals.

◄ At the crime scene, investigators collect biological samples using swabs like cotton buds. Stored in a perfectly clean tube, often containing a preservative, the swab is chilled to make sure that DNA in the sample does not decay before it is analyzed.

Identifying the dead

When a tsunami ripped across the Indian Ocean on Boxing Day 2004, thousands of people died. Towering waves tore away clothes and possessions that might have shown who the victims were. Within a few days the corpses were so swollen in the tropical heat that even close family members could not recognize them. Governments turned to DNA to identify the dead. They took samples from victims' bodies, and from survivors who had lost relatives. Matching the DNA profiles allowed a family to bury a lost parent or child.

Perfect proof?

Investigators use DNA not only to match suspect to crime, but also to identify bodies that are beyond recognition. DNA is also sensitive: just a forty-millionth of a drop of blood can produce a result.

However, DNA tests are not fool-proof. Samples can be polluted with DNA from other sources, confusing the result. On small islands where everyone is related, the DNA is very similar and DNA profiling is not such a reliable way of proving guilt.

► Working with tiny samples of bodily fluids, serologists mix DNA from a suspect or crime scene with a chemical 'amplifier'. In a process called polymerase chain reaction (PCR), the chemical increases the amount of DNA in the sample, until there is enough to test.

Teeth and bones

How do you identify a bag of bones? Skulls and skeletons are often all that is left of the victims of crime once fire or animals have consumed the flesh. Figuring out who was burned or buried is the job of forensic anthropologists. Using teeth and bones as clues, they can estimate sex, age, height and race. Forensic dentists can even give a skull a name if they can compare the teeth to dental records.

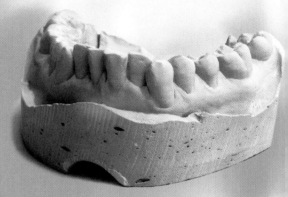
▼ The casts that dentists take when fitting dentures give forensic anthropologists an ideal way of identifying rotted or burned bodies. Most often they use dental records or X-rays, or – where these do not exist – descriptions from friends and family.

▼ By assembling a skeleton, scientists can estimate how tall a crime victim was when they were alive. Where some bones are missing, the most reliable guide to height is the femur (thigh bone). On average our height is 3¾ times the length of this bone.

▶ At the scene of a major fire or other disaster, forensic dentists use portable X-ray machines to record the teeth of the bodies. The X-rays reveal gaps (dark patches) and fillings (light patches). Matching the patterns to dental records helps identify victims.

Bleached or blackened bones

Human bodies do not last long. In warm weather it takes animals and bacteria just one month to pick every scrap of flesh from a corpse in the open air. Fire is an even quicker way to blot out identity – an intense fire can reduce a body to bones in an hour or less.

To the untrained eye skeletons are little more than grisly signs of death. However, to a forensic anthropologist they are like an open book, filled with information about the living.

Young or old?

To estimate age, anthropologists look at the growth of teeth and bones. Children's first teeth appear at around six months. These grow and change continuously until the last permanent teeth grow at around the age of 13.

For teenagers and adults, bone growth is a better age guide. At birth bones are soft and separate; they grow harder and fuse (join) together in a predictable order. The long bones, for example, have separate ends until the age of about 13, when they fuse together. The clavicle (collar bone) is the last to fuse, when the person is about 28 years old. For older people, forensic anthropologists also look at the shape of the ends of the ribs. These become more hollow and spiky as age increases. Wear and tear on the joints and teeth is also a good guide to a skeleton's age.

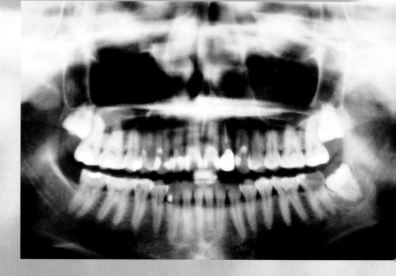

A woman's pelvis (hip bones) must be wide enough for a baby's head to pass through during childbirth. Men have much narrower hips, and the difference in the size of these bones makes them the easiest way to judge the sex of a skeleton.

Marks on the skeleton

Skilled anthropologists can read much more from a skeleton. From the points where muscle meets bone they can judge how strong the person was. Distinctive patterns of wear may hint at the work they did. Injuries and a few diseases also leave recognizable marks on the skeleton.

Man or woman?

Looking at the shape of bones, rather than their size, reveals the sex of the victim. The pelvis (hip bones) shows this most clearly, for women have much wider hips than men.

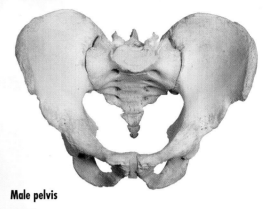

Female pelvis

Male pelvis

Looking at the skull

There are less obvious clues to be found on the skull. For example, its shape can hint at the race or ethnic background of the dead person. White people have round skulls, with jaws directly below their eyebrows. People with African ancestors have more oval skulls, and faces that slope back from the jaw to the eyes.

Open wide!

Teeth are the last parts to rot or burn, so a skull – or just one jaw – may be enough to identify a body. Dentists look for filled, bridged, capped or missing teeth, and compare them to dental charts or X-rays. This method of identification is especially valuable in fires or transport disasters, where anthropologists try to match scorched bodies to a list of known victims.

Measuring the skull can help an anthropologist tell whether victim was black, white or Asian. The height of the skull is also important. Added to the length of the back, hip, leg and foot bones, shows how tall the dead person was.

Making faces

Without flesh, or eyes, or hair, a skull gives no clues to the appearance, personality and character of the face that once smiled from it. Yet the bones of the skull are the foundations of the face. By building on them with clay or with software, forensic sculptors and computer artists can reconstruct the faces of the dead. Their lifelike images may enable witnesses to identify a murder victim.

Reconstruction starts

Attempts to recreate faces from skulls of the dead started in Germany in the 1880s. Anatomists (scientists who study the human body) used needles and knives to measure the depth of flesh on the faces of corpses. With this knowledge, they were able to mould the right thickness of clay on to casts of the skulls to create a likeness. This method of reconstruction continued unchanged for more than a century, until computer technology made it possible to recreate faces more precisely.

Three-dimensional scanning

Using a three-dimensional (3-D) scanner, the position and shape of every bone can be recorded. The result is a 3-D model that can be viewed from any angle.

Today, information about the thickness of muscle, fat and skin on the face now comes not from corpses but from living subjects. Computer tomography (CT) scans create 3-D images of both bone and soft tissue such as muscle. This makes it possible to measure flesh depths without needles or knives. Not only is this safe and painless, it also gives more accurate results than measuring corpses. In death, muscles relax, and the face sags.

Merge and match

Technicians merge the scan of an unidentified skull with the CT scan of a person of the same age, sex and race. Then they 'warp' the skull of the CT scan, stretching or squashing it until the two virtual skulls are the same size. Warping the CT skull also creates an accurate simulation of the flesh layers on the dead person's skull

◀ Computer modelling applies layers of virtual 'flesh' to a scan of a skull. Once the model is complete, it is easy to make the face look fatter or thinner, and older or younger.

▲ Just as a facial reconstruction builds faces from the skulls of the dead, so photofit images can create a likeness of the living. By making a 'jigsaw puzzle' from a library of face parts, witnesses build up pictures of suspects or missing people.

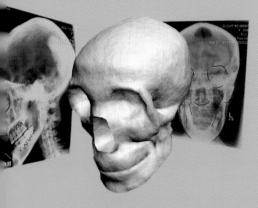

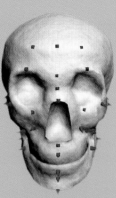

◀ Rebuilding faces from a skull is based on science and years of experience. The bones of the face provide no clues as to the shape of the lips, ears, eyes and nose, so forensic artists must guess what the features looked like.

▲ To reconstruct a face, X-ray photographs are taken of the skull and a replica is made to show the shape.

▲ Pins are placed at key points where muscles attach.

▲ Muscles are then added in the right places to the skull.

▲ Finally, the cartilage, skin and eyes are added.

The result is a virtual view of the face as if created from white clay. Technicians then add colour and texture using a 'colour map'. This is a photograph of someone investigators believe resembles their subject. Like the CT scan, the texture wraps around the surface of the model.

▶ After building a face, technicians make a plaster cast from the clay model. Plaster is white, so to make it look more lifelike, skilled artists carefully paint the surface of the clay.

Finishing touches

The computer then calculates the appearance of every point on the face, building a view from one angle or from many. This gives either an ordinary portrait with photographic realism, or a virtual head that witnesses or relatives can view on-screen from any angle.

▲ When making computerized reconstructions of faces, technicians can add spectacles, hair, beards and moustaches from a menu. Without these clues, it is often difficult to recognize even the faces of relatives or close friends.

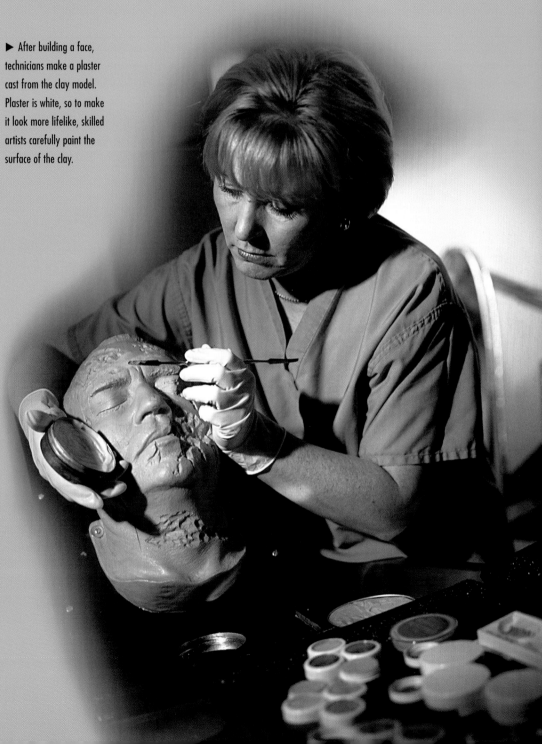

Matching fingerprints

A record of every criminal's fingerprints seems like a great way to identify suspects. However, a fingerprint collection is useless unless detectives can easily search it for prints that match those they find at the crime scene. Detectives found a way of doing this more than a century ago. Today, computer databases take seconds to compare a crime scene print against millions of criminal records.

Fingerprint breakthrough

When a hospital in Tokyo, Japan, was burgled in 1879, the police were sure they knew who was responsible. But the man they accused was saved from punishment by a friend, Henry Faulds (1843–1930). Visiting the crime scene, he spotted a dirty fingerprint the burglar had left on a wall. Faulds pointed out that none of the patterns on his friend's fingertips matched the thief's print. It was the first time fingerprints had been used in a criminal case.

▼ Detectives scan prints they find, and the automatic fingerprint identification systems (AFIS) computer tries to match any minutiae with those of known criminals' prints. The system presents the closest matches on screen so detectives can compare them with those of the suspect.

▼ Fingerprint classification systems plot where ridges end or fork (shown here as round blobs). Fingerprint examiners would be confident that they had identified a suspect if a dozen of these 'minutiae' from the criminal's record matched a print from the crime scene.

► Traditional police files record suspects' fingerprints by pressing or rolling the inked fingertips on a card. To make searching possible, fingerprint examiners split up these ten prints, and classify each one individually.

Classifying fingertips

To make searching practical, detectives divide the prints according to their basic shapes: loops, arches and whorls (see left). Then, each group is split according to the number of ridges, their direction and other details.

Classifying the fingerprints in this way means the number of possible matches could be reduced from thousands to dozens. Searching the prints becomes more practical – just as the alphabetical arrangement of a dictionary lets you find a word quickly.

Computer searches

Today, computer systems do much of the searching. Detectives scan the hands of convicted criminals, and for each fingertip, computers analyze and encode the 'minutiae'. These are the distinctive features, such as the points where ridges branch, fork or end.

When detectives find a print at the crime scene, they scan it, and the computer tries to match its minutiae with the prints on file. The closest matches are presented for detectives to make the final comparison.

Automatic fingerprint identification systems (AFIS) can search a million fingerprint records in less than a second. The system in use in the USA contains more than 40 million prints, and 700 are added each day.

Ramirez is caught!

In 1985, the people of Los Angeles, USA, were terrified when a serial killer prowled their city. In August, a man he had shot survived, and described the killer's car. Police found it, and checked for fingerprints. They found just one, but using the city's AFIS, matched it to Richard Ramirez. His picture was flashed on television and he was arrested the next day. At his 1988 trial he was found guilty of 13 murders, and sentenced to death.

► By storing fingerprints as digital records, like this one from the French police service, fingerprint examiners can search a million records in less than one second.

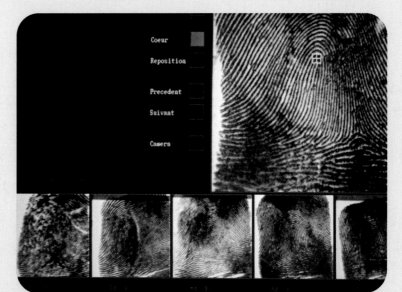

Unknown villain

When there is no obvious culprit for a crime, detectives start eliminating people from their enquiries. By excluding everyone who seems unlikely to have committed the crime, they narrow down their investigation to the few people who might possibly be guilty. When even this approach fails, they may turn to offender profiling — a method of identifying criminals by studying how they commit their crimes.

▶ In the incident room at a police station, officers plot sightings of a suspect on a wall map. Phone calls and sightings of cars are all recorded to build up a picture of where the suspect has been. This helps them to narrow down their search area.

◀ When criminals dash from a crime scene, witnesses may not see enough of them to provide a full description. Nevertheless, the smallest details about weight, age and fitness can help police to piece together a profile of their suspect.

Catching a killer

A woman is gunned down in a busy city street. Witnesses who heard the shots saw a young man run quickly from the scene. He dived into a car and drove away at speed. Evidence a the crime scene tells detectives little, so how do they find the killer?

When the investigation begins, everyone is a potential suspect. The police need to eliminate whole groups of people to narrow their search. They start with the sex of the attacker. Half the population is female, so already they have reduced the number of suspects by 50 per cent. Because the killer was a young man the police can rule out anyone under 16, or over 40. He sprinted from the scene – so the suspect is reasonably fit. Detectives may also eliminate people who cannot drive, because he escaped in a car.

Offender profiles

Forensic scientists have tried to improve on this traditional approach by looking at what sort of people commit crimes. From the few clues they have, they try to build a profile (a shape or pattern) of what the criminal was probably like.

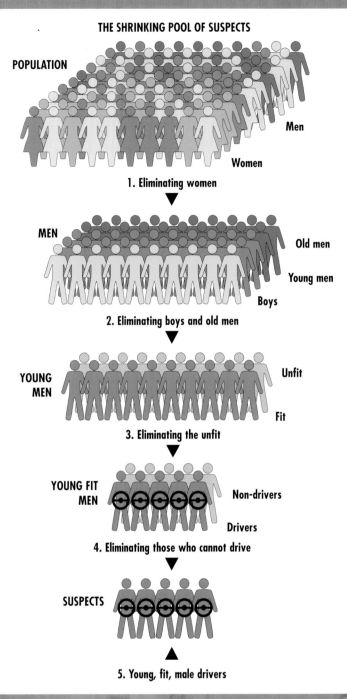

THE SHRINKING POOL OF SUSPECTS

POPULATION

Men

Women

1. Eliminating women

MEN

Old men

Young men

Boys

2. Eliminating boys and old men

YOUNG MEN

Unfit

Fit

3. Eliminating the unfit

YOUNG FIT MEN

Non-drivers

Drivers

4. Eliminating those who cannot drive

SUSPECTS

5. Young, fit, male drivers

Catching the New York bomber

One of the first profiling cases led to the arrest of New York's 'Mad Bomber', who planted 30 bombs in the city over 16 years. In 1957, when conventional attempts to catch the bomber failed, detectives turned to psychiatrist Dr James Brussel.

Brussel told them the bomber was a man, as female criminals rarely use bombs. He sent bombs and threats to Con. Edison, the city's power company, so maybe he was sacked by the company, or hated it for some other reason. His handiwork on the bombs showed he was neat and careful. The formal language of his letters suggested he was foreign, and probably east European, because people from this region had used bombs in the past. Dr Brussel even predicted that when he was arrested, the bomber would be wearing an old-fashioned suit, buttoned up.

From this, a secretary at Con. Edison found the records of a man who had been injured years before. He fitted the doctor's description perfectly and when police swooped on his home, they found him wearing his suit, buttoned up!

► Identifying a suspect is usually a process of elimination. Gender, age, physical fitness and abilities can all help the police pinpoint a criminal within a social group. By eliminating large sections of the population from their enquiries, the police are able to focus their resources on the remaining section, and find their suspect.

► House-to-house enquiries, like this one from France, help the police identify criminals. The police ask standard questions of each householder to build up a picture of the local community and find out if their suspect is known there.

Proof of guilt

'He's the man. I am sure. I saw him with my own eyes.' Witness statements like these persuade us of suspects' guilt, but can we really trust them? Research shows that witnesses find it hard to pick villains out from line-ups and albums of mugshots. Blurry security camera pictures make it even harder. Other modern crime-busting aids, such as lie detectors, seem equally unreliable witnesses.

Never forget a face

We all trust our memories, especially when we look back on an experience as dramatic as a crime. However, identifying someone we have seen for only a moment, perhaps weeks before, is more difficult than it seems.

In a line-up, or identity parade, a suspect stands in a row of similar-looking people. Out of their sight, an officer asks the witness to pick out who they saw. Some choose correctly, but wrong identification is common.

Facing up to the truth

Mugshot albums do not have a much better track record. Witnesses are asked to look at photographs of previously convicted criminals who match the description given to the police. The person the witness picks out may then become a suspect – even if there is no other evidence against them.

▶ Closed-circuit television cameras can record city dwellers as they go about their daily business. They show the police if a suspect was in the area when a crime was committed.

◀ The film from closed-circuit television (CCTV) is routinely used as evidence for the police. It can show them if a person matching the suspect's description was involved in the crime.

Photofit faces

The police also use composite photos. A witness describes who they saw commit the crime, and an officer puts together a picture of the suspect's face from a menu of photographs of mouths, eyes, ears, chins, noses and hairstyles. Police officers then use the 'photofit' picture to search for a suspect. Newspapers often publish the composites to encourage members of the public to join the hunt.

► The polygraph, or lie detector, monitors changes in a suspect's sweating, heartbeat and breathing. These changes may indicate they are lying. However, tests have shown that smart criminals can beat the lie detector.

Protecting the innocent

Despite their problems, all these methods and machines, such as closed-circuit television (CCTV), can help to catch criminals. Used wisely and fairly, police officers can jail those who are actually guilty. To take full advantage of them, detectives must first realize that memory is unreliable. To protect innocent people, they must look at the whole picture, and not rely on identification alone.

SUMMARY OF CHAPTER 2: WHO IS IT?

Identifying criminal and victim

Much of an investigator's work is concerned with identity. Who committed the crime? Whose body has been found?

An 'ABO' blood test can help find an answer. It shows to which of four groups someone's blood belongs. If blood at a crime scene is not the same group as a suspect's blood, police know they have arrested the wrong person.

DNA testing is an accurate way to check identity. Forensic scientists extract DNA from blood or tissue samples. Testing produces a string of numbers unique to that person. Matching numbers from a crime scene sample and a suspect greatly increases the possibility that the suspect committed the crime.

Some other trusted methods of identifying people are surprisingly unreliable: witnesses make mistakes when they look for suspects' faces in mugshots or line-ups.

Crimes with no suspect

When there are no witnesses, no blood samples and no photographs for detectives to go on, identifying a suspect is especially challenging. Investigators start by eliminating everyone who could not possibly have been at the scene. Occasionally they try offender profiling, using what they know about the crime to guess what sort of person did it.

Fingerprints also lead detectives to an unknown suspect. If detectives find prints at the crime scene, they search their files of previous offenders to find a match. As these files grew, searches took longer, but today computers speed up the process.

Investigators cannot use fingerprints to identify long-dead or burned victims. Instead they look at the size and shape of bones and teeth. These are clues to age, weight, sex and race. Teeth can tell detectives exactly who they have found – but only if they have dental records. If these are not available, forensic anthropologists use crime victims' skulls to recreate their faces. With clay or computer software they build up a likeness – though they have to guess the ears, eyes, lips and nose.

Go further...

 Find out about the history of fingerprinting and how it helps to solve crimes at: http://www.cyberbee.com/whodunnit/fp.html

Discover basic information on the structure and function of DNA as it relates to DNA fingerprinting by visiting: http://protist.biology.washington.edu/fingerprint/dnaintro.html

Use maths and forensic science to work out the relationship between the length of your foot and your height: http://www.cyberbee.com/whodunnit/foot.html

KFK Genes & DNA by Richard Walker (Kingfisher, 2003)

 Forensic anthropologist
Studies human remains to estimate the age, sex, height and other facts, and to help identify the body.

Forensic entomologist
Investigates insect activity connected to a crime, and uses a knowledge of insect life cycles to find out the date and time of death.

Forensic pathologist
Studies the bodies of crime victims both inside and out. Also tries to decide what killed them.

Forensic technician
Helps forensic scientists by preparing evidence, maintaining equipment and recording results.

 Explore the cells while discovering more about crime, forensic science, forgery and international policing: Greater Manchester Police Museum, Newton Street, Manchester, M1 1ES, UK
Telephone: +44 (0) 161 856 3287
www.gmp.police.uk/about_gmp/history.asp

Help solve The Great Train Robbery and find out more about other crimes from the casebooks of the Thames Valley Police Force: The Force Museum, Sulhamstead House, Sulhamstead, Reading, RG7 4DU, UK (Visits by appointment only.)
Telephone: +44 (0) 118 932 5748
www.thamesvalley.police.uk/about/museum

CHAPTER 3

Crime lab

Sometimes, all it takes to solve a crime is a single strand of hair, a fleck of paint, or a drop of blood that is too small to see without a microscope.

Forensic scientists look for this, and much more, at a crime laboratory: a specialist centre where technicians can analyze, study and test the evidence found at crime scenes. In the smallest labs, a couple of technicians might do all the work. But bigger laboratories have specialists who concentrate on just one field of forensic science.

Our tour of the crime laboratory starts in the autopsy room. This is where medical examiners, called pathologists, carry out detailed studies of the bodies of crime victims, and people who die in suspicious ways. Not only can they determine how people died, but also when they died.

The autopsy

With its white tiles, bright lights and shiny benches, the autopsy room looks like an operating theatre. But instead of surgeons, forensic pathologists wield the scalpels. In autopsies, bodies are cut open to find out how a person died. An autopsy is the most detailed part of the post-mortem (after-death) investigation. This is a thorough study that includes photographs and X-rays of the body, and a complete inspection of its appearance.

Starting on the outside

Because every suspicious death is different, no two autopsies are exactly alike. However, most begin with the careful removal of clothes from the body and their examination for evidence. The pathologist weighs the body and takes a good look at its outside appearance. Cuts, bruises, scars and identifying marks must all be noted. These are dictated into a tape recorder.

The external examination and X-ray photographs guide pathologists when they start to dissect (cut up) the body. If the cause of death is not clear, it is usual to do an autopsy of the whole body. By following standard procedures, pathologists investigate all the organs of the body to establish the cause of death.

A general autopsy

The pathologist starts this by opening the body cavity using razor-sharp blades and saws or bone-cutters. A slit, or a T- or Y-shaped cut up the front of the body, brings the internal organs within reach. The pathologist removes the organs, taking careful note of any injuries before weighing them individually. Taking samples of fluid and tissue from each organ makes it possible for toxicologists (see page 52) to test for the presence of drugs, poisons or alcohol. The skull does not escape attention either: to study the brain it is necessary to cut around the bones of the head.

Looking for signs

Pathologists look for subtle signs that are easy to miss. For example, strangulation often causes no obvious injuries on the outside of the body: the tell-tale signs lie beneath the skin. To be sure that their subject was strangled, pathologists must drain all blood from the neck and carefully peel back layers of tissue. This reveals the tiny bruises that confirm the crime. Stabbing victims also need special attention to trace the path of the knife through the flesh.

Essential notes

The pathologists' studies are useless unless they write down what they have found. Their autopsy reports can help expose murders disguised as suicide, or they can free someone wrongly accused of killing by showing that the 'victim' died of natural causes.

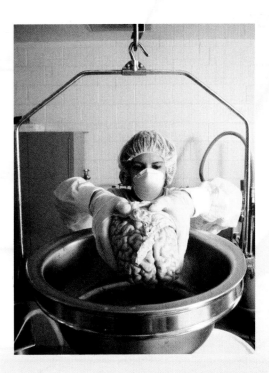

▲ Pathologists weigh body parts they remove during an autopsy. Many diseases cause a change in weight of the body's organs, so this information must appear in the autopsy report.

◀ Pathologists do not work alone. An assistant from the morgue (body storage area) lifts the corpse on to a stainless steel table, and helps with jobs, such as sawing open the skull, that do not need the pathologist's skill.

How did they die?

If only corpses could speak, they could tell investigators just how they died. Even autopsies cannot give these silent witnesses voices, but they can discover some of their secrets. From their bumps and bruises, cuts and burns the forensic pathologist can often piece together the story of a crime victim's last moments. Along with evidence from the crime scene, and statements from witnesses, the post mortem examination sorts out natural deaths from accidents, murder and suicide.

The manner of death

Deciding how someone died is important because it suggests whether or not a crime has been committed. If the death was natural or suicide, police may have nothing to investigate.

Pathologists call this important decision the manner of death – the way or method in which the victim died. They choose from just four possibilities: natural death, accidental death, suicide or homicide (deliberate killing).

The cause of death

Before making a choice, the pathologist looks for the cause of death: what ended this person's life? Was it an injury, such as a stab wound that caused massive bleeding? Perhaps electrocution stopped the heart. Or was it fatal illness, such as a sudden stroke? The answer may seem obvious, but pathologists must consider every possible cause of death, and decide which is the most likely.

Suicide or murder?

For example, in the burned-out shell of a car the police find the charred body of the owner. An empty petrol can and the lighter in his hand tell the rest of the story. The pathologist's first step might be to look for soot in the lungs, because people who are burned to death breathe in smoke. Clean lungs would suggest that the victim was dead before the fire was started, and did not kill himself. Though burning a corpse destroys many clues, a closer examination might reveal the true cause of death. A skull fracture, for example, is all the proof that is needed to start a murder hunt.

The stealthy killer

Often the tell-tale signs of murder are not obvious at all. It is common for sick, frail, old people to die of natural causes, but pathologists study their dead faces very carefully. Slight bruising around the mouth and nose, or pin-prick sized spots of blood beneath the skin of the neck suggest that they may have been smothered with a pillow. Such a discovery might send the police looking for a family member who stood to gain by their elderly relative's death.

▼ By the time the pathologist packs her crime scene bag, she may already have suspicions about how the victim died. There may be further clues about this scattered around the crime scene, but collecting them is the job of SOCOs. The pathologist's real work begins when she studies the body in the autopsy room. There she can look for internal evidence that even fire could not destroy.

▲ A blow to the head does not always cause damage that's obvious, like the swelling on the right of this scan. Often a pathologist has to make a microscopic study of slices of the brain to spot the bleeding that caused death.

Sealing off the crime scene prevents the curious from trampling on clues that might reveal the cause of death.

Careful handling of the corpse helps preserve evidence.

The pathologist examines the body's position and surroundings to help her understand how the victim died.

A SOCO's discovery of tyre tracks suggests that the death might be suspicious, because another vehicle left the crime scene.

Though fire-fighters may destroy evidence through their work, their first priority is to rescue anyone caught in the blaze.

Dust

Wool and synthetic fibre

Polyester fibres

Weave

Trace evidence

A brutal attacker, called 'the Fox', scrapes his car at a crime scene. It leaves a fleck of paint 115cm up a tree. Microscopic study shows the paint colour is 'harvest yellow'. Thousands of cars are painted this colour, but detectives track them all. One has a scratch 115cm from the ground. The owner confesses. These crumbs of paint, fibres and glass, called trace evidence, link the car, victim and crime scene in a chain of proof.

Swapping evidence

The attacks committed by the Fox in 1984 show the truth of an important idea, that every contact leaves a trace. Called 'Locard's Exchange Principle', after the French detective who devised it, it has a simple meaning: at the scene of every crime there will be traces left behind by the criminal. Criminals also carry away traces they picked up at the crime scene. In other words, there has been an exchange, or swapping, of trace evidence.

Collecting and studying traces

Trace evidence is often too tiny to see with the naked eye, so detectives collect it with sticky tape or with a forensic vacuum cleaner. It is then studied under a microscope. There are five types of microscope.

Ordinary microscopes light trace evidence from behind, so they show clear details in only thin or transparent materials. Polarized light microscopes use filters to block out light. Many kinds of evidence, such as glass, 'undo' the blocking, so they appear bright. Stereoscopic microscopes have twin eyepieces and show the evidence in three dimensions. Comparison microscopes make it easy to study two similar pieces of evidence to see if they match. Electron microscopes reveal incredible surface details on paint flakes, hair and fibres.

◀ Whether it is found in dust, or woven into fabric, the shape of a thread enables detectives to identify the fibre. However, fibre shape and colour are useful clues only if they are unusual. White cotton, for example, is so common that it rarely helps link a suspect to a crime. These fibres are shown magnified thousands of times.

▶ A forensic vacuum sucks up trace evidence and collects it on a paper filter. Magnifying the filter with a microscope shows up the tiniest specks of dust.

How paint proves guilt

Putting a flake of paint under the microscope can show how many coats there are and the colour of each one. Police can match car paints with makes, models and years, as in the example of the Fox. House paints can also offer useful clues. For example, if police find a flake of paint stuck to a suspect's crowbar, they might compare it with the paint on the window of a burgled house. A match would suggest that the suspect was the burglar.

Looking closely at glass

Although one piece of glass looks much the same as another, a forensic laboratory can identify a tiny glass flake by measuring its light-bending power and its density (the weight of a standard piece). These tests could, for example, match a flake of glass found on a hit-and-run victim with the broken headlights of a car. If the pieces are large enough, fitting them together like a jigsaw puzzle would also prove the driver's guilt.

▶ When two vehicles collide, each leaves traces of paint on the other. Here an investigator carefully pulls a paint flake loose from a crashed car. Its colours, and the order in which they were painted, will identify the make, model and possibly the age of the other car involved in the accident.

▼ To detectives, dirty fingernails do not mean bad hygiene: they are a vital source of trace evidence! When victims of violent crime struggle with their attackers, they may scratch off enough skin for DNA testing (see pages 26–27).

Fantastic fibres

Fibres from clothes look remarkably different under the microscope. Natural fibres such as wool, cotton and linen have distinctive shapes that make them easy to recognize. When dyed, their colours provide extra clues which help detectives find a match. For identifying artificial fibres, such as nylon, chemical tests are used.

Dirty proof

Mud, filth, dirt, dead insects – and live maggots. When cleaning the house, we sweep, scrub and spray to be rid of these unwanted things, but forensic scientists actually collect them. Natural materials form a special kind of trace evidence. Matching samples taken from the suspect, victim and crime scene can prove a link between them, and living things, such as pollen, can also provide a calendar to show the season or time of a crime.

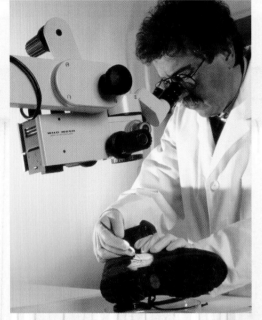

▲ With the aid of a stereoscopic microscope, forensic scientists can spot tiny traces of dirt even on apparently clean shoes taken from a suspect. The dirt will be evidence of guilt if it matches samples of soil at the crime scene.

▼ Forensic entomologists (insect experts) keep libraries of dead flies (top of the page) and their maggots (bottom). When found on corpses, a fly's stage of development allows detectives to estimate the time of death.

Mud as evidence

As criminals flee from a robbery, the wheels of their car spin in the dirt. When police find the car, they find mud in the wheel arches. Matching it to mud at the crime scene shows the car was used in the robbery.

To confirm that two samples come from the same place, they are studied under a microscope and the particle size, shape and type are compared. For example, land sand has sharp edges but beach sand is rounded.

C. nana
Tivoli 15.06.93
1993 ml 3.

C. nana
17.03.1993
1990

C. nana
03.1993

Picking flowers

Seeds and other parts of plants are used in a similar way. Microscopic examination helps identify what plant the material came from. Suspicions would increase if the seeds of an unusual plant found at the crime scene were found on a suspect's clothes.

Plants make pollen in spring and seeds in summer. So by studying dirty clothes, detectives might prove not only that a suspect visited a crime scene, but also when they were there.

Hair samples

Like clothing fibres, hairs have special shapes and colours. These properties help forensic scientists match them, or at least guess where they are from. If you look at human hairs under a microscope you will see some striking differences. Hairs from the scalp are round in cross-section; those from the armpit are oval; and hairs from beards are roughly triangular. Hairs also store a record of lifestyle, pollution and chemicals. For example, tests on the hairs can reveal if a suspect has a history of drug use.

The bugs that cleared a sailor

Soon after death, flies may lay eggs on corpses and the life-cycle of the grubs that hatch show when victims died.

A Hungarian ferry captain was accused of murder after a body was found on his ferry. An autopsy found fly eggs and grubs on the corpse. A forensic entomologist gave evidence that the eggs were from a kind of fly that was active by day. The captain only came on duty at 6pm, and the victim must have died earlier than this. Therefore the captain could not have been the murderer, and he was freed.

▼ Magnified many thousands of times, tiny pollen grains (coloured purple here) from different plants look unique. Their shapes help detectives figure out what plants a suspect or victim might have touched.

Computers and crime

Today's wired world seems like the perfect playground for criminals. Corrupt programmers hack into banks' computer systems, steal money, and then vanish. However, escaping justice is becoming much harder as forensic science catches up with cyber-crime. Computer experts know how to find clues hidden on hard disks, and can track down those who use the internet.

More computers, more crimes

The spread of computers has made old crimes easier: for example, traditional blackmailers can now make their demands by e-mail. It has also led to new crimes. Computer viruses did not exist 25 years ago, because too few people owned computers.

Computer fraud

Viruses that throttle the internet make headlines, but forensic computer experts spend most of their time studying computers seized in crime such as fraud. Recovering data from them is a special challenge,

▲ Fraudsters trick computer users into revealing their secret passwords. Spam e-mails ask victims to confirm them by typing them in on bogus websites that look identical to the official bank site. Criminals then collect the passwords and steal their money.

Computers become infected

Viruses are tiny programs that copy themselves. They are spread by e-mail, and run invisibly, causing damage to computers. To find virus writers, computer security experts trace the spread of the 'infection'. They also look for clues in the virus code: often programmers hide their 'signatures' in lines of code.

▼ Computer experts keep an eye out for hacker attacks by watching the flow of data and messages on the internet. A sudden surge in volume may show that a new virus is spreading rapidly. Unless these 'infections' are stopped, computers worldwide can choke on the junk messages the virus creates.

Melissa virus

In March 1999, millions of computer users opened 'an important message' apparently from a trusted friend. In fact it was a virus, which caused over US$80 million damage. The internet service provider AOL discovered that a subscriber had uploaded the virus, named Melissa, to one of its message boards. By looking at computer logs, AOL found the telephone number the virus author used to dial in. This clue led the FBI to a New Jersey programmer, called David Smith, who was jailed for 20 months.

...ecause just switching a computer ...n can erase valuable evidence. ...o the technicians make an exact ...opy of the computer's hard disk ...without starting up the computer. ...y working on this copy, they ...eave the original untouched.

The way computers store data ...makes the technicians' job easier. ...When villains 'erase' files from a hard ...disk, the data is not destroyed: the ...le just becomes invisible. Even ...riminals who completely wipe out ...etters and e-mails that might prove ...heir guilt are not safe. Computers ...tore multiple copies as temporary ...les. Electronic detectives can track ...own and read these duplicates.

Online fraud

...n 1994, Vladimir Levin hacked into ... Citibank computer in New York.

▲ When e-mails spread the 'I love you' virus in May 2000, the internet ground to a halt, and businesses lost billions. Investigators traced the attack to a 23-year-old Filipino, Onel de Guzman, who created it for a college project. There is no law against making viruses in the Philippines, so de Guzman escaped prosecution.

Without leaving his desk in St Petersburg, Russia, he electronically transferred more than $5 million into his own accounts. Detectives tracked him down by allowing him to continue his illegal transfers and following the money and phone calls back to Russia.

Such cases are very rare, because banks now protect their central computers with more care. Today, fraudsters find it easier to target online banking, by 'phishing' – sending out millions of spam e-mails to lure bank customers to fake web sites. These sites often look exactly like an online bank, but are completely fake. Customers are asked to enter their security codes and passwords. With this information, the criminals can then empty that customer's account.

▼ Information sent on the internet is not secure unless the browser page displays a tiny padlock symbol. Users who type in their credit card numbers on non-secure pages risk having them stolen. Thieves then fake credit cards with the same numbers and can run up huge bills.

Credit Card

EXPRESS

Bombs and fires

Bombs and arson (deliberate fires) turn buildings and vehicles into charred ruins and rubble. Amazingly, though, even the fiercest blasts and flames do not burn up everything. Picking through the smoking embers, forensic experts often find enough of the device that triggered the destruction to trace the criminals who placed it.

Tongues of flame

Buildings are designed to resist a blaze, so arsonists start their fires with accelerants – fast-burning fuels, such as petrol. To avoid being trapped in the flames themselves, some also use a timing device. An electric timer or even a candle resting on oil-soaked rags will delay the fire until the wick burns low.

A bigger bang

Bombs can be sophisticated or simple, but the results are usually the same: destruction and often death. The crudest bombs are made from low explosives. For example, even fertilizer and diesel fuel can make an explosive mixture.

Terrorists prefer high explosives such as Semtex – a handful of which is enough to blow up a car. Setting off any explosive is not as simple as it might appear. Most will not explode without detonators. Triggered by a timer, these devices ignite with a tiny bang that then sets off the main charge.

◀ Despite the destruction that a terrorist car bomb causes, the pattern of damage can lead investigators to the spot in the vehicle where the explosives were placed.

Investigation

Detectives investigating fires and bombs first need to find what caused the destruction. A burst gas pipe, for example, could cause similar damage to a terrorist bomb.

To trace a fire's cause, detectives need to establish where it started. Often the only instruments they need are their eyes. Arson crime scenes may contain accelerants. To find small traces they use electronic 'sniffers' – devices that detect them.

Patterns of soot and blast lead to the 'seat' of the fire or explosion. This is where the destruction began, and it is here that investigators hope to find the device that lit the flames or triggered the explosion.

To identify the explosive or accelerant used at the crime scene, SOCOs collect evidence in air-tight containers. At the crime lab, forensic scientists use microscopes to search the evidence for traces of explosive. They also run chemical tests on any vapour found inside the containers. Their instruments reveal the unique signatures of the chemicals that bombers and arsonists use.

◄ In suspicious fires, police and firefighters work together to make buildings safe and check that everyone is accounted for. They then cordon off the area to ensure that only essential personnel work at the crime scene.

▼ A fingertip search at a bomb site can turn up traces of batteries, wires and a timer. Comparing these traces with a computer database of similar devices from previous attacks puts police on the trail of the bomber.

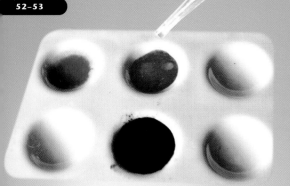

▲ Forensic testing kits change colour when mixed with drugs. In this demonstration, blue shows crack cocaine, black shows cannabis and red shows that amphetamines are present. Urine tests for drugs are much more sensitive than this, because they must spot the tiny quantities that pass through a drug user's body.

▼ Mailed inside letters, the deadly bacteria anthrax killed three Americans in 2001. Scientists who studied the DNA of the germ discovered that it had been grown in a US Army research centre. Nobody was ever caught for the crime.

Drugs and poisons

In thrilling true crime stories from the past, cunning murderers slipped deadly powders into their victims' drinks. They also seemed to get away with it, but not any more. For today's poisoners cannot beat the tests of toxicologists. These forensic specialists look for toxins – alcohol, drugs and poisons – in human blood, urine and flesh.

Sensitive tests

In the toxicology laboratory, rows of machines process samples taken from suspects and corpses. These instruments can detect a drug diluted five billion times: the equivalent of two aspirin tablets dissolved in an Olympic swimming pool. No wonder poisoners stand so little chance of avoiding detection! In fact, toxicologists hardly ever see poisons used as murder weapons any more. Most cases of poisoning are accidents, such as drug overdoses or people drinking weedkiller by mistake.

▲ Poisoner Crippen was the first criminal to be caught by newly invented 'wireless'. The captain of the ship on which he was travelling recognized him and radioed the Canadian police.

Looking for drugs

Toxicologists work on samples of body fluid, or organs such as the liver, that are removed during an autopsy. But not all of the samples are from dead subjects. Toxicologists also work with the police to stop people from using illegal drugs. Law officers carry out simple tests when an arrest is made. A five-minute 'dip and read' urine-testing kit changes in pattern or colour if it is likely that an illegal drug is present. If this test shows a 'yes' result, a nurse would take a blood sample for further testing in the lab.

Two-stage tests

There, testing is done in two stages. The first makes sure that the sample contains drugs; a second test works out the exact amount. In modern labs, toxicologists use testing machines like small robots. These suck up the samples, prepare them, run the tests, and then present the results on a computer screen. This technology is vital in alcohol testing. Analyzing samples from drunk drivers makes up most of the work of the toxicology lab, and testing by hand would take far too long.

Catching Doctor Crippen

When Doctor Hawley Crippen (1862–1910) announced that his unfaithful wife had left London to return to the USA, her friends became suspicious. After Crippen himself vanished, police dug up the cellar of his house and found his wife's body. Tests showed a lethal dose of the drug hyoscine. Crippen was spotted on an Atlantic liner, with his attractive secretary disguised as a boy. The couple were arrested on their arrival in Canada, and Crippen was hanged for murder four months later.

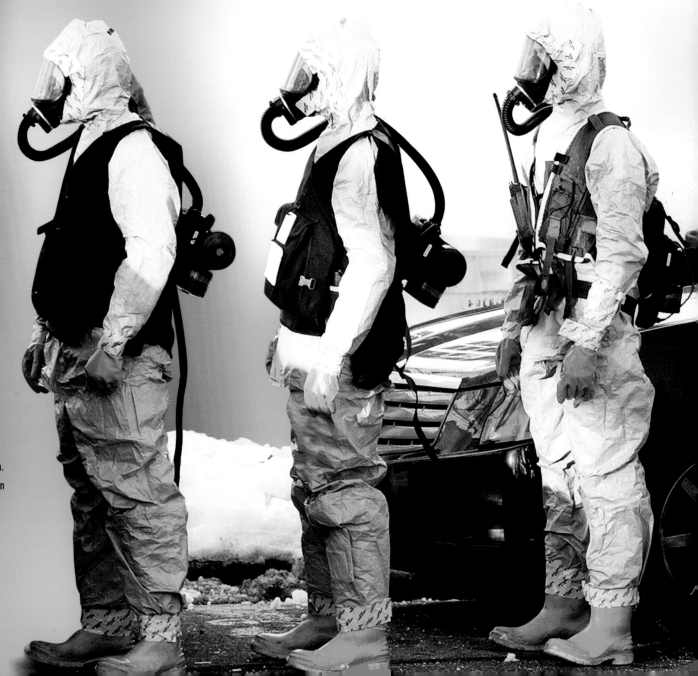

▶ Police found this bag of heroin when they raided a drug dealer's flat. Toxicologists are more likely to come across the drug when addicts take too much of it. It shows up in the blood, hair and organ tissue of those who die from an overdose.

▶ Easy detection stops murderers using poison, but terrorists do not fear discovery. They use poison to cause panic and disruption. They succeeded in 2004 when a poison scare shut down much of the US Congress (government). US Marines wore protective suits to check for ricin, a deadly nerve poison, that was sent to an American politician.

Weapons

In a murder investigation, finding a weapon brings the detectives on the case a step closer to the killer. Though knives and clubs rarely leave identifying marks on victims, guns provide detectives with more useful evidence. Spiral ridges cut inside the barrel of a gun, known as rifling, mark bullets with grooves that are as distinctive as fingerprints. Pulling the trigger stains the killer's hands, also making identification easier.

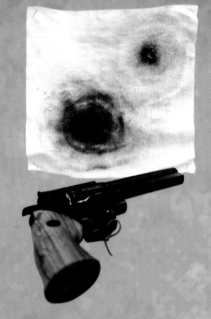

▲ By test-firing a gun from different distances, firearms experts can estimate how far apart a killer and victim were. At close range a gun leaves a bigger deposit of gunpowder around the wound.

► SOCOs handle firearms with great care – not just to preserve evidence, but also because guns are deadly when loaded. Here an investigator makes a gun safe by removing the magazine of bullets. She wears gloves to avoid putting her own fingerprints on the weapon.

Which gun fired the fatal shot?

From a bullet's shape, firearms examiners – forensic experts who specialize in guns and their use – can guess *what* sort of gun fired it. But finding out exactly *which* gun is more difficult. This is done by looking at the grooves in the bullet's surface that are caused by rifling. These ridges, cut in the gun's barrel, spin the bullet to keep its flight straight.

Matching bullet and gun

The rifling marks have more value as evidence if investigators find a suspect's gun. To judge whether this gun shot the fatal bullet, they load and fire it.

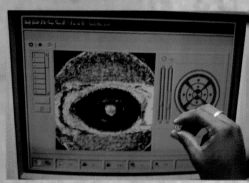

▲ The US *Brasscatcher* database records images of cartridge cases from guns used in crimes. If a cartridge case from a new crime matches one on the database, the same gun has been used again.

► New crime scene kits allow police to wipe a suspect's hands with a swab soaked in a special chemical, and see immediately if they have fired a gun recently.

◄ In a gun test by US police, a firearms examiner aims the weapon safely into a water tank. Comparison of the bullet with those found at the crime scene will show whether the suspect fired this gun.

Dirty hands

Guns leave another kind of mark that is extremely useful to detectives in tracking killers. A small amount of the explosive in the cartridge case always sprays out from gaps in the gun's mechanism. This is called gunshot residue. Some of this residue will end up on the gunman's hands. So testing a suspect's hands for gunshot residue can prove that they fired a gun in the previous six hours.

Catching the bullet safely in water or soft material preserves the tell-tale grooves. A comparison microscope allows the firearms examiner to see whether the marks match those found on the bullet taken from the victim's body.

When there is no suspect weapon, firearms examiners may see if the grooves match those on bullets fired in previous crimes. They do this using a computer program which stores and compares rifling marks.

Cartridge cases

Bullets are not the only useful kind of firearms evidence. For each bullet fired, there is also a cartridge case. This metal tube contains the explosive charge that propels the bullet. Pulling a gun's trigger forces a hammer on to the end of the cartridge, detonating the explosive inside. The hammer leaves a mark as distinctive as the groove on the bullet, and this can be matched in a similar way.

Most guns eject a cartridge case each time they are fired. Where the cases fall can help detectives work out where the suspect was standing when they pulled the trigger (see page 15).

▼ Shotgun pellets spread as they fly from the barrel. The size of the pattern they form shows the distance between the gun and target. This X-ray shows the result of a close-range shooting.

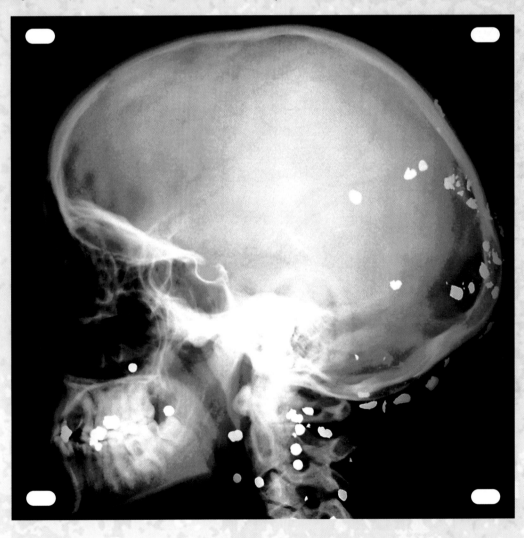

Fakes and forgeries

They look like £20 notes. They feel like money and they are printed on thick, crispy paper like all banknotes. But forged or fake paper money is worthless. Worse, you could face jail if you spend it. Money is the oldest and easiest target for forgers, but today these criminals are as likely to copy valuable documents, art, credit cards, DVDs, watches or even designer clothes.

Trademark pirates
Dior, Nike, Rolex, Adidas, Prada: designer labels stand for quality and style, but how can you be sure that what you are wearing is the real thing? Do you really care? Forgers are making a fortune selling us bogus goods that look just like the brands they imitate.

▼ The pirate DVDs these soldiers are destroying in Ecuador sell for a fraction of the cost of the real thing. The poor-quality recordings do not put off customers who buy nine fakes for each genuine disc sold.

◄ Passport fraud is big business, but making a passport that looks genuine is not easy. More often, forgers buy stolen passports and change the photo and name to those of the person who is buying it.

Cheats at the till

People are less easily fooled than these machines, though very good forged notes are difficult to tell from the real thing. To recognize the counterfeits, document examiners (forensic forgery specialists) use microscopes and chemical tests. Tracing the type and source of the paper and ink may lead them to the forgers. By plotting where criminals used identical notes, they can follow the progress of the gang, which should hopefully lead to their arrest.

Fashion victims

Detecting fake designer goods becomes more and more difficult as forgers become cleverer. When anti-piracy detectives swoop on clothing factories they now take with them fashion industry experts to examine every stitch. Clothing companies are helping too, with hard-to-forge labels and hidden security features that can only be spotted if one knows where to look. But as long as people crave the look without the price, the trade seems sure to continue.

Printing money

Money is very different from clothes. Nobody wants a fake note in their wallet, so banks try hard to make their notes impossible to copy. They use tiny printing, special inks, foil strips, holograms and watermarks – images built into the paper that appear only when you hold the note up to the light.

Nevertheless, forgers still copy money, using many different printing methods and papers. None quite matches the special printing presses that banks use, though some come close. Colour photocopies were good enough to fool change-making machines, until the banknotes and machines were altered to spot the fakes.

▼ In the chaos that wars cause, forgers thrive. US soldiers found these sheets of uncut banknotes when they invaded Iraq in 2003. The criminals who printed them hoped to pass them off as real when Iraq's banks changed over to new notes later in the year.

Not so fantastic plastic

Plastic bank cards are easier to forge than money, because each bank uses different patterns – whereas every £20 note looks exactly the same. Criminals search constantly for ways to defeat card security features. For example, dishonest workers in shops and restaurants swipe genuine cards through a pocket-sized card-reader to steal security details from the magnetic strips. Recording the same data onto fake cards ensures they are accepted at the till.

To combat card crime, document examiners look for links between cards, such as a tiny fault in the embossed name. This enables them to identify cards made by the same forgers.

Bogus masterpiece

Faking the work of a famous painter is tougher than forging a credit card. To make pictures that will fool art experts, forgers must copy not only artists' styles, but also their materials. Modern paints are very different from

▲ To test whether an 'old' painting really is genuine, scientists need to remove only the tiniest flecks of paint. Studying the paint using techniques such as mass spectroscopy and infra-red spectroscopy may reveal what it is made from.

those that artists used a century ago, so analyzing paint can reveal a painting's age.

Though a convincing fake can sell for millions, not all art forgeries fetch such high prices. Because of the difficulty of faking the work of great artists, many art forgers tackle easier projects. They make cheaper artworks that experts will not study so closely. For example, as many as half of all 'ancient' Greek bronze statues are probably fake, because they are easy to make. They sell well to private collectors who are less likely to spot a fake than the staff of galleries who have access to instruments to verify the materials used.

◄ English forger Tom Keating (1918–1984) tricked the art world by painting hundreds of fakes. Some still hang undetected on gallery walls. Keating did not do it for the money. A failed artist, he turned to forgery to get his own back on the critics who disliked his paintings.

SUMMARY OF CHAPTER 3: CRIME LAB

The need for a laboratory

Much of the forensic scientist's work is done in a laboratory. One of the most important tasks there is to examine the bodies of people who have died in suspicious circumstances. In autopsies, forensic pathologists look closely at the outside of bodies, then cut them open to study their organs, flesh and fluids.

What happens at the laboratory?

Forensic scientists study trace evidence left behind by criminals. SOCOs collect traces with sticky tape or special vacuums and examine them under the microscope. The natural world is a good source of useful trace evidence. Soil, plants and insects found on corpses can tell scientists much about the crime committed.

Computer software and hardware is used to find evidence stored electronically. Scientists here target traditional criminals or hackers who spread havoc online.

Other forensic scientists specialize in fire and explosions. Experts sift evidence from scenes of devastation to see what fuelled the blast or flames.

They search for traces of a timing device, that might hold vital clues about the identity of who started the fire.

In the laboratory, toxicologists test body fluids for evidence of drug abuse or poison. Much of their work aims to prove the guilt of drunk drivers.

If guns are found, specialist firearms examiners are called in. They fire seized guns and compare the bullets with those found at the crime scene. Marks and scratches can show if the same gun was used in the crime. Cartridge cases also carry marks that can tell a similar story. Gunshot residues on criminals' hands may prove that they pulled the trigger.

Pollen grains can provide clues for forensic scientists

Go further...

Find out how dental records can help identify a victim at:
http://www.cyberbee.com/whodunnit/teeth.html

Become a forensic scientist and use chemistry to help identify the mysterious white powder:
http://www.cyberbee.com/whodunnit/powder.html

Discover how to find any hidden files on your computer by visiting:
http://whyfiles.org/014forensic/computer_data.html

KFK Mummies by John Malam (Kingfisher 2003)

Document examiner
Examines suspicious documents for changes, decides whether they are genuine or fake, and compares handwriting and signatures.

Electronic caseworker
Unravels the information stored in suspects' computers, handheld organizers and mobile phones.

Firearms examiner
Checks, tests and compares weapons and ammunition used in crimes, and analyzes evidence to find out how suspects used their guns.

Toxicologist
Tests body fluids and tissues for traces of drugs and alcohol.

Use forensic techniques to identify fingerprints, footprints, DNA and hair samples to solve a crime:
Thinktank, Millennium Point, Curzon Street, Birmingham B4 7XG, UK
Telephone: +44 (0) 121 202 2222
www.thinktank.ac.uk

Glossary

assassin
A murderer, especially one who attacks by surprise.

bacteria
Tiny living things, some of which cause disease in animals or plants.

barrel of the gun
The tube-shaped front end of a gun that guides a bullet towards its target.

blackmailer
Someone who has information that will damage their victim, and who demands money to keep it secret.

body bag
A zip-up bag for carrying a dead body and preserving evidence clinging to it.

cartridge case
The brass cap that holds together a bullet and the explosive charge needed to fire it.

CCTV
Short for closed-circuit television: a security camera.

chain of custody
A list of all the people who have looked after a piece of evidence between the crime scene and the court.

chain of proof
A series of linked facts or evidence.

corpse
A dead body.

court
The place where a trial is held.

cross-section
The shape of something when cut in half.

crowbar
A hooked metal bar used for prising things open.

database
A computerized list.

dental charts
A chart showing the condition of each of a person's teeth.

DFO
Short for 1,8-diaza-9-fluorenone, a chemical that makes fingerprints on paper glow.

dip-and-read urine test
A testing strip that changes colour when dipped in urine if the person has recently taken a drug, or there is glucose or blood present.

drug
A medicine or chemical sometimes used illegally to create an altered state of consciousness.

evidence
An object, information or a mark that tells investigators about a crime.

evidence card
A piece of cardboard to which detectives stick evidence, such as fingerprints.

explosion
The blast caused by a bomb or uncontrolled burning of gas or fuel.

FBI
Short for Federal Bureau of Investigation: the national detective agency of the USA.

fibre
A strand of thread.

fingertip search
A very detailed search in which detectives run their hands over an area to check for evidence.

genes
Patterns of simple chemicals that control the shape and growth of every living thing. Parents pass on genes to their children.

guilty
To blame for a crime.

hacker
Someone who breaks into a computer system and changes or steals computer data, either to commit a crime, or create mischief.

identity parade
A chance for a witness to pick out a suspect from similar-looking people.

innocent
Not to blame for a crime.
See also guilty.

judge
An official who is in charge
of a court, and who
decides how a criminal
should be punished.

jury
A group of ordinary
people who listen
to evidence at a trial,
and decide whether
a suspect is guilty
or innocent.

lie detector
Nickname for a polygraph,
a device used to measure
changes in a suspect's
sweating, breathing and
heartbeat when they
give untrue answers
to questions.

light bending power
The ability of a transparent
substance such as glass to
bend a beam of light
passing through it.

line-up
See identity parade.

magnetic brush
A brush containing a
magnet, for dusting
fingerprints with iron
powder without actually
touching them.

mugshot
Slang for an identity
photograph – usually
of a criminal.

on-line
Connected or provided
using the internet.

pathologist
A medical doctor who
studies diseases and
injuries and their causes.

pattern evidence
Any kind of evidence
where the objects or
marks themselves are
less important than the
pattern they form.

piracy
Robbery at sea, but now
used to mean the copying
of someone's work, or of
a company's products.

pulse
The throbbing in
someone's veins and
arteries caused by the
heart's pumping action.

rifling
Spiralling ridges cut inside
a gun barrel. Rifling spins
bullets, making them hit
the target more accurately.

scale
An object such as a ruler,
with marks a fixed distance
apart, to make size and
distance more obvious.

scalpel
A very sharp knife used
by surgeons.

scene of crime officer
An investigator who works
at the scene of the crime.

SOCO
Short for scene of crime
officer.

spam
Unwanted 'junk' e-mail,
often containing a hidden
program that can damage
the computer it runs on.

suspect
Someone whom
investigators believe might
be to blame for a crime.

suspicious death
Any death that police
believe may have been
caused by a criminal
act such as murder.

trial
The process of deciding
whether or not a suspect
is guilty, and – if they
are – how they should
be punished.

ultraviolet radiation
An invisible form of
energy similar to light.

vital signs
Signs such as warmth
and a pulse that show
that someone is alive.

VMD
Short for vacuum
metal deposition, a way
of making fingerprints
show up on shiny
surfaces such as plastic.

Index

Acknowledgements

The Publisher would like to thank the following for permission to reproduce their material. Every care has been taken to trace copyright holders. However, if there have been unintentional omissions or failure to trace copyright holders, we apologize and will, if informed, endeavour to make corrections in any future edition.

Key: *b* = bottom, *c* = centre, *l* = left, *r* = right, *t* = top

Cover *left* Science Photo Library (SPL)/Michael Donne; cover *centre background* SPL/ Mehau Kulyk; cover *centre foreground* SPL/ Mehau Kulyk; cover *right* SPL/ Tek Image; page 1 Corbis/Reuters; 2-3 Corbis/Ron Sachs; 4-5 Getty News; 7 Getty Stone; 8-9 Alamy/Wesley Hitt; 8*bl* Corbis/Mark Peterson; 9*tr* Getty News; 9*br* Getty Stone; 10-11 Alamy/Shout; 10*tr* Getty Stone; 11*br* Corbis/Reuters; 12*bl* Associated Press; 12*cr* SPL/Michael Donne; 13 SPL/Michael Donne; 14*tr* Alamy/Plainpicture; 14*b* Alamy/Carphoto; 15*bl* Getty News; 15 Getty Stone; 16-17 Corbis/Mark Peterson; 16*bl* SPL/Pascal Goetgheluck; 17*tr* SPL/Alfred Pasieka; 18*t* Alamy/Imagesource; 18*tr* SPL/Volker Steger; 18*b* Alamy/Comstock; 19 Alamy/JG Photography; 19*b* Alamy/Mikael Karlsson; 20*bl* SPL/Volker Steger; 20*r* Getty; 21*br* Corbis/Charles O'Rear; 22 Rex Features; 23 Digital Vision; 24-25 SPL/Andrew Syred; 24*bl* Corbis; 24-25*c* Corbis/Robert Patrick; 25*tr* SPL/Eurelios; 25*b* SPL/Peter Menzel; 26-27 Imaging Body; 26*tr* Getty Photographer's Choice; 26*b* SPL/Tek Image; 27*br* SPL/Colin Cuthbert; 28-29 Corbis; 28*tr* Alamy/Pat Behnke; 28*bl* Getty/Photographer's Choice; 28*br* Corbis; 29*t* Alamy; 29*b* SPL/Mauro Fermariello; 30*l* Corbis/Sygma; 30*cr* SPL/Mauro Fermariello; 30*br* SPL/ Michel Viard; 31*b* SPL/ John McClean; 32 SPL/Mauro Fermariello; 32-33 Corbis; 33*tl* Corbis/Reuters; 33*b* SPL/Philippe Plailly; 34*l* Alamy; 35*t* Corbis/Reuters; 35*b* Corbis/Sygma; 36*l* Corbis/Reuters; 36-37*c* Corbis/Reuters; 37*r* Alamy/Brand X; 38 SPL/Peter Menzel; 39 SPL/Volker Steger; 40-41 Corbis/ San Francisco Chronicle; 41*tr* SPL/Custom Medical Stock; 43 SPL/Gca; 44-45 SPL/Eye of Science; 44*tl* SPL/David Scarf; 44*tcl* SPL/Eye of Science; 44*bcl* SPL/Eye of Science; 44*bl* SPL/Eye of Science; 44*br* SPL/Mauro Fermariello; 45*tr* SPL/Mauro Fermariello; 45*bl* Alamy/Mikael Karlsson; 46-47*t* SPL/Pascal Goetgheluck; 46*tl* PL/Volker Steger; 47*br* SPL/Susumu Nishinaga; 48-49 Getty Imagebank; 48*tr* Alamy; 49*t* Corbis/Sygma; 49*br* Alamy/Comstock; 50-51 SPL/Michael Donne; 50*cl* Corbis/Francois de Mulder; 50-51*b* Alamy/Blue Shadows; 51*r* Associated Press; 52-53 Corbis; 52*tl* SPL/Mauro Fermariello; 52*cr* Getty News; 52*bl* Corbis/CDC; 53*tr* SPL/Gusto; 53*b* Corbis/Reuters; 54*tr* Alamy/Mikael Karlsson; 54*bl* SPL/Mauro Fermariello; 54*br* Getty News; 55*tl* Getty News; 55*tr* Getty News; 55*b* SPL/ISM; 56-57 Corbis/Sygma; 56 Getty News; 57*tl* Getty News; 57*b* Getty News; 58 SPL/Andrew Syred; 58*tr* SPL/ Volker Steger; 58*b* Rex Features; 60*l* Imaging Body; 62-63 Rex Features; 64 Corbis/Reuters

The Publisher would like to thank the following illustrators:
34–35*tr* Encompass Graphics; 42–43*r* Jurgen Ziewe